PRUDENT WITH MONEY

[simple steps to become financially whole]

BY

JOSE G KIM

TABLE OF CONTENT

DISCLAIMER

The data contained in this book is for instructive purposes as it were. No portrayal is being made that any atmosphere will or is probably going to accomplish benefits.

Misfortunes like those examined in this book.

The previous exhibition of any exchanging framework or on the other hand approach isn't really characteristic of future outcomes.

By examining this book, you concur that my company and I are not answerable for the achievement or on the other hand setback of your exchanging business.The thoughts I'm going to introduce are ones that

I've gained from different Thinkers(see the atmosphere-knowledgements segment) and I don't promise to be the first fountain head of them.

BOOK DESCRIPTION

Regardless of where you are in your financial journey, you can learn something from Get Good with Money.

A successful pre-kindergarten educator with a substantial nest egg when a recession and advice from a dodgy visor caused her to lose her job and fall into a massive financial hole, during which time the outline of her ten-step formula for achieving financial security and peace of mind began to emerge.

In the book Get Good with Money, the author explains the powerful idea of creating wealth through financial wholeness. This is a real, doable, and exciting alternative to methods for getting rich quickly or managing money in a way that is too complicated.

- **A simple way to set up a "noodle budget," look at and organize your spending, and make a plan to reach your goals.**

- **A diagnostic tool that tells you if your problem is that you don't make enough money or that you spend too much, and** gives you advice on how to fix either problem.

- The top strategies for putting away cash for emergencies, major purchases (like a new home, car, or trip), and long-term investments like stocks and bonds.

- Advice and next steps for managing your credit, automating your bill-paying, savings, and investments, and figuring out how much life, disability, and property insurance you need.

- Long-term strategies for providing for your heirs and meeting your financial objectives

A wonderful resource for establishing secure financial practices and putting your money to work, prudent with Money will set you on the path to a life of wealth and success (and legacy).

CHAPTER ONE

LEARN WHAT FINANCIAL WHOLENESS IS AND HOW TO BUILD A BUDGET.

Truthfulness in Finances

A personalized path to financial wellness that actually delivers

Half of all Australian families questioned (independent PWC and KPMG polls) reported suffering financial stress, and this was the case regardless of household income.

We think that banks have been unfair to most families for far too long with their one-size-fits-all approach to home loans, which often leads to more debt and higher interest rates and can put stress on marriages and family ties.

This is the first step on our Path to Financial Wholeness, where we will work to fix the problem one Australian household at a time.

Our Financial Wholeness Journey will take care of our customers' biggest money worries, so they can rest easy:

Gives you a complete picture of your financial condition in the context of your aspirations and current way of life.

Offers a clear path forward, sound financial counsel, and a confidential accountability partner to track your progress each month.

Describes a strategy for accumulating wealth outside of conventional salary-based methods.

There are 10 parts to a complete financial picture.

Take the quiz at getgoodwithmoney.com to find out your financial wholeness score, which takes into account the following factors:

1. Budget

2. A Strategy for Financial Reserves

3. Debt Resolution Strategy for Debt

4. Credit

5. A Comprehension of Monetary Strategy

6. Putting Away Money for the Future

7. Insurance

8. Price tag

9. Professionals in the Financial Sector

10. Arranging Your Affairs After Your Death

As Jose put it, "it's not about all of us arriving at the same location at the same time." Financial wholeness depends on your specific life stage and financial situation. For example, let's discuss estate planning. In your twenties, this might

mean adding your parents or a close relative to your bank accounts and buying a life insurance policy that lets your loved ones take care of your financial obligations if you die. It's okay if not everyone becomes financially independent, as Tiffany put it, but she stressed that everyone can become financially whole.

DISGRACE AND AFFECTIONATE FINANCIAL RESULTS

Jose didn't start working for financial stability until she was 35 years old, and she now feels embarrassed and ashamed about the fact that she didn't address some things or take actions to get them under control sooner. You see, the problem is, a new beginning is still a new beginning. There's always a chance that you'll wrap up a job faster than expected, regardless of when you start working on it. As Tiffany observed, "So many people don't get up, so they never get there."

Given that your headlights can only see around 60 feet in front of you, you might as well never go

on a road trip. "Once you've driven the first 60 feet, the next 60 feet are wide open!"

Jose "When I made a financial mistake, I felt ashamed. I didn't realize how destructive this feeling is until I read an article about how shame is one of the most dangerous emotions because it causes isolation, thrives in seclusion, silences you because it grows in silence, keeps you in darkness, and tells you that there's something wrong with you. Shame is a liar, and it's a terrible place to live. "

CHAPTER TWO

SPEND LESS AND SAVE MORE

When asked, "What is BUDGETING" Many people struggle to define the term.

Budgeting is the tactical implementation of a business plan. In order to achieve the objectives outlined in a company's strategic plan, a detailed,

descriptive road map of the business plan is required, coupled with a set of metrics and indicators of performance.

Strategy Translation: Setting Goals and Allocating Resources

When developing a plan to put into action an organization's overarching strategy—its mission, vision, and goals—it is necessary to take four factors into account.

1. amount at your retail establishment.

2. The company can get customers to spend more money by offering more products and services, finding new suppliers, advertising its products and services, and so on.

3. The effectiveness of the techniques must be tracked and evaluated using the right metrics, such as the average weekly spending per customer and average price changes as inputs.

4. Lastly, you should set goals for what you want to do by the end of the set amount of time. These

goals should be measurable and have a set time frame, like increasing sales by a certain amount or number of units.

Budgeting's Ends and Means

There are several reasons why creating a budget is essential for any organization.

One, it helps with the preparation for the real procedures.

The procedure teaches managers not only how to predict possible changes and plan for them, but also how to deal with problems as they come up.

The second function is to coordinate the group's efforts.

Managers are incentivized to network with and learn about the other aspects of the business by creating a budget that helps them see how their departments and teams contribute to the whole.

Sharing your plans with other supervisors

A key social part of the process is sharing plans with managers so that everyone knows their role in the company and can work together to achieve common goals. This makes it easier for people to talk to each other about their plans and activities that help the company grow.

Encourages business leaders to work hard to meet financial targets.

When pay and performance are tied to the budget, managers' attention is brought back to the budgeting process, and both they and their subordinates are more likely to reach their goals.

5. Managers can keep tabs on finances by comparing spending to projections.

Take stock of how well managers are doing. Managers can learn how well they are doing in terms of achieving their goals thanks to the information provided by budgets.

Various budgetary structures

Operating, capital expenditure, and cash budgets all feed into the master budget, which then makes a planned income statement, balance sheet, and cash flow statement.

In first place, the operating budget Revenues and expenses are budgeted for on a regular basis, and the budget is broken down into areas such as salaries, benefits, and other operating costs.

Capital expenditure

Capital budgets are used to distribute funds, control risks in decision making, and set priorities and are generally requested for the acquisition of substantial assets like property, equipment, or IT systems that put a significant strain on an organization's cash flow.

Cash-based budget

The timing of payments and receipt of cash from revenues are factored into cash budgets, which assist management in keeping tabs on the company's cash flow and making informed decisions about whether or not more money needs to be raised or whether or not it can get by with the money it already has on hand.

Although some large corporations may take a whole fiscal year to complete their budgets, the vast majority of businesses begin their budgeting process four to six months before the start of the financial year and do monthly budget setting and variance analysis. Communication between executives, setting goals and targets, making a detailed budget, putting together and updating the budget model, reviewing and approving the budget by the budget committee, and finally putting the budget into action are all steps along the way.

Construction and design budgets

A budget is a plan that details how and where a set amount of money will be spent over a given time period or on a specific item (like a building). A budget is defined as follows in the CIOB Code of Practice for Project Management, Fourth Edition:

A budget is a financial and/or quantitative statement, prepared and approved before a defined period for the purpose of attaining a given objective for that period. In other words, it is the "quantification of resources needed to achieve a task within a set timeframe, within which the task owners are required to work."

Budgets for building projects should be established as early as feasible, with careful attention paid to ensure that they are realistic and based on solid facts. In the RIBA Plan of Work 2013, the term "project budget" refers to "the client's budget for the project, which may include the cost of construction as well as the cost of specific goods necessary post-completion and during the project's operational usage."

It is possible to create a project budget by:

Income and cost estimates throughout the duration of the project.

Analogy to Other Projects

To take stock of the available resources

Requirements analysis before design.

Analysis of potential layouts during the concept stage

The project budget is set by the client, which is different from the cost plans made by a cost consultant, which tend to focus on the cost of construction.

The client's overall project budget may consist of:

The price tag on building it?

Acquiring a piece of land or some other piece of property

Spending on Interest and Fees for Financing.

We're conducting a site survey.

Home furnishings, appliances, and other mechanical accompaniments

The whole expense of packing up and transferring everything, including the salaries of any employees who must relocate,

Extra-curricular agreements

A Safety Net

Paying for expert advice

Devaluation of the currency

An if-then clause

VAT.

It's important to keep an eye on costs because it's common for the project budget and project brief to change as the project goes on.

The client must make it crystal clear to the cost consultant which costs are under the consultant's purview and which costs remain under the client's jurisdiction.

Here Are the Simple Steps to Take When Creating Your Own Budget

You need a budget if you want to keep your spending in check and make progress toward your financial goals.

Even though the word "budget" may make you think of being tight with your money, a personal or family budget is just a summary of your income and expenses over a certain time period, usually one month.

Instead of seeing a budget as a hindrance, think of it as a tool to help you achieve your financial goals by laying out how much money you expect to earn, how much you will need to spend on fixed expenses like rent and insurance, and how much you will have left over for things like entertainment and eating out.

Why Is It Necessary to Have a Budget?

You can plan how much of your income you will spend or save each month with the use of a written monthly budget, which is a useful financial planning tool.

Putting together a budget may not sound like the most exciting thing to do, and it may even be scary for some people. However, it is important for keeping your finances in order because it forces you to find a balance between your income and your expenses. without being willing to be completely transparent about your income and expenses.

Ultimately, your new budget will reveal your monthly income and expenditures, as well as where your money is coming from and going to.

A Step-by-Step Guide to Making a Budget

In order to make a budget that serves your needs and allows you to live a comfortable and happy life, you need to have a solid understanding of your present spending habits, your financial resources, and your top priorities.

Get a strong budget template in place before you start plugging in your actual numbers for costs and income.

You can use a piece of paper and a pen to create a budget, but a monthly budget spreadsheet or a budgeting app is much more convenient and time-saving because of the dedicated fields for income and expenses in different categories and the built-in formulas that calculate your budget surplus or shortfall for you.

1. Assemble your financial records.

Gather all of your financial documents, including:

The bank statements

Financial planning

Current utility bills

Paystubs and W-2 forms

- **1099s**

Payments on Credit Cards

Financial records from the previous three months

Mortgage or auto loan statements

One of the most important steps in building a budget is calculating a monthly average of your income and expenses, so you should have as much of this data at your disposal as possible.

2. Calculate Your Earnings

If you receive a regular paycheck from which taxes are automatically withheld, use the net income (or take-home pay) amount to estimate your monthly income. If you work for yourself or get money from other sources, like child support or Social Security, figure out how much this total is each month.

If you have a fluctuating income (maybe due to seasonal or freelance work), one strategy for budgeting is to use the amount you earned in the month with the lowest earnings as your starting point.

3. Document your regular monthly costs.

Make a comprehensive list of all the monthly outlays you anticipate, such as

Monthly rent or mortgage?

Loans for vehicles

Safety Nets

Products for the Kitchen and Pantry

Basic Services

Theatrical Value

Maintenance of one's own person

Consuming Prepared Meals

Children's Services

Transportation expenses

Transportation

Funding for Higher Education

The Money You'll Save

Take a look at your credit card bills, bank statements, and receipts from the past three months to itemize everything you've spent.

4. Sort your expenses into fixed and variable categories.

Fixed expenses include mortgage or rent payments, auto payments, internet subscriptions with a set monthly fee, trash collection, regular child care, and any other significant outlays that tend to remain consistent month after month.

Include savings and debt payments as fixed expenses if you want to save or repay a set amount each month.

Expenses like these are known as "variable" and will fluctuate from month to month.

Products for the Kitchen and Pantry

Motor Fuel

- Theatrical Value

Consuming Prepared Meals

Gifts

Don't let unexpected costs derail your monthly budget by failing to plan for them ahead of time.

Begin by putting a dollar amount on your fixed monthly bills, and work backwards to determine how much you can reasonably expect to spend on everything else.

Review your credit card or bank statements from the past two or three months to get a ballpark figure for how much you spend in each area.

5. Total Your Monthly Revenue and Expenses

If your income is greater than your outgoings, you have a surplus that can be spent toward other goals within your budget, like saving for retirement or paying down debt.

If you find yourself with more money coming in than going out, you may choose to embrace the "50-30-20" budgeting theory, in which 50% of your income goes toward "needs," or basic spending, while another 30% goes toward "wants," and the other 20% goes toward savings and debt reduction.

If you spend more than you earn, you need to reevaluate your spending habits.

6. Finding ways to lower your variable expenses, such as eating in more often or eliminating them, like your gym membership, is a good idea if your outgoing costs exceed your incoming revenue.

You may need to cut your fixed spending and boost your income if your expenses are considerably greater than your income or if you have a large amount of debt.

If your income and spending columns are both equal, it means that all of your income has been counted and is being used to pay for or work toward something else.

The Best Way to Spend Money

After creating a budget, it is important to keep close tabs on your spending, ideally recording each day's costs in the same spreadsheet or software that you used to create your budget.

It's better to spend a few minutes a day recording your expenses than to spend an hour at the end of the month trying to figure out where all your money went.

If you aren't sure how good you are at budgeting, you could use the envelope system. With this method, you set aside money for different expenses and then don't buy anything in that category until the money in the envelope is gone.

As you use your budget, keep track of how much you've spent in each category; once you hit your limit, you'll need to either cut back on that type of spending for the month or reallocate funds from another.

When creating a budget, remember that the number one rule is to never spend more than you earn in a given month.

Revisit your financial plan and make adjustments.

Make a date with yourself every few months to sit down with your budget and make sure it's working for you now that you've adjusted your priorities, changed jobs, relocated, and/or added children to your family. If you have your figures entered into a program or website, you can easily experiment with your budget categories to find out where you can cut costs or give greater weight to certain items.

Keep in mind that your budget shouldn't determine your needs.

Budgeting Advice

Once you have a working budget in place, you can modify it to fit your needs and goals.

- **If your income is based on commission, you need to save heavily for market downturns.**

If you are having trouble making ends meet because you only get paid once a month, try breaking up your paycheck into weekly chunks and putting the money you were planning to spend on non-essentials into a separate account.

- **Only make purchases on a credit card if you know you will be able to pay off the full balance at the end of the billing cycle.**

Keep an eye on significant, infrequently occurring expenses, such as insurance premium payments, and adjust your monthly budget accordingly.

- **Use budgeting tricks, such as a cash-only budget, if you know you have a spending problem in certain areas.**

- **Prioritize saving goals in your budget before increasing expenditure once you've reached a point where your expenses are below your income.**

- **Invest some time in expanding your knowledge of money management in order to get the most out of your resources.**

CHAPTER THREE

PAY OFF YOUR DEBT

One of the main reasons I am a millionaire in my 30s as a black woman in America without an inheritance or special advantages is that I am a saver, which is one of the first and most critical stages toward reaching financial independence.

My own family has shown me that saving is not innate for everyone, but that it is a blessing that it is innate for me, and the good news is that it is absolutely a skill that can be learned! I have always been a saver and like stacking my pennies. My brother, who is ten years older than I am, first took money from me when I was six years old and he was sixteen.

Tips on how to put money aside for retirement:

***Make a rough estimate of your monthly income, your fixed (food, housing, transportation, and telephone), and your variable (entertainment, cable, and clothing) living expenses, and then subtract your net income from your net fixed and net variable expenses to determine your discretionary income.**

*Set up automatic deposits from your paycheck into your savings account as the next step. This is a crucial step because once you've automated your savings, money starts to accumulate rapidly. Promise yourself that you won't touch your savings unless it's an absolute emergency, and if you do, you'll put the money back in your savings within three months.

*Whatever motivates you to continue saving like a squirrel, do it. Your goal could be to save six months' worth of living expenses for an emergency fund, a down payment on a home, or funds to purchase a vehicle.

I started with a basic Citibank savings account because I could easily set up my automatic transfers and monitor my progress within the same banking interface. Citibank also had a robust rewards program at the time that allowed me to double and triple my monthly earnings by having multiple active accounts, so the interest I was paying was offset by points.

The ability to take advantage of unexpected opportunities is one of the main benefits of saving aggressively. At age 24, I had no plans to buy an apartment in New York City, but I found a great deal and happened to have the exact down payment amount of $25,000.

facilitating smart and uncomplicated investments.

***Get your money invested today.**

Get a portfolio of investments that is always being watched and changed to fit your risk level.

Squirrel Save's AI builds and monitors your portfolio with you in mind, around the clock, using the most recent market data and zero human bias.

There is no need for knowledge, experience, or tough choices.

The AI in SquirrelSave will automatically manage and rebalance your portfolio to get you the best predicted returns for the level of risk you set.

You can start with absolutely zero requirements. If you don't have much money to put toward your savings goal, don't worry; SquirrelSave AI can handle a single dollar.

No more excuses! Add or withdraw funds at any moment.

CHAPTER FOUR

LEARN HOW TO EARN

(INCREASE YOUR INCOME).

Getting Out Of Financial Difficulty

Mortgages, student loans, credit cards, personal loans, bills, and more have left the average American with $92,727 in debt in 2020, according to Experian. This is the highest amount ever recorded in the United States. Members of Generation X owe a whopping $140,643, followed by Baby Boomers ($97,290) and Millennials ($87,448).

You probably have debt if you are here reading this, and the only way to get out of the financial hole you've dug for yourself is to change your debt behaviors and start digging.

Eight solutions to the burden of debt are provided below.

The Pluses of Excavation

Financial stress can make it more difficult to save money, stick to a budget, or even write a shopping list to keep you on track at the store, all of which can have a negative impact on your health, according to a study by Capital One in 2020.

Financial freedom can boost self-esteem, confidence, and long-term savings, as does reducing stress and anxiety.

The "avalanche" and "snowball" methods are two strategies often recommended by financial experts for prioritizing the repayment of debt. The avalanche method entails paying off loans and credit cards with the highest interest rates first, by making as much as possible toward them while making only the minimum payment on your other loans.

1. Listening to the Noise.

Put your loan statements, bills, and budget on the kitchen table, along with anything else you can think of that pertains to your finances, and begin adding up. This is the first step if you've been trying to make unread bills disappear by dumping them.

Basic payments will include loan or credit card payments and expenses for necessities like electricity, heat, and water. If these already significantly exceed your net income, you will either need to make drastic lifestyle changes (sell the property, move into a smaller apartment, find a second job), declare bankruptcy, or both.

2. Journey of Atonement

Not all loans are created equal, so it's important to establish a debt hierarchy and formulate an attack strategy. High-interest debt should be at the top of this list, followed by low-interest debt that is not tax-deductible and then tax-deductible debt.

Make an emergency fund and hide your credit cards; cancel all but one card; go on a cash-only diet; and stick to your repayment plan.

3. Check your credit score and report any errors or unfavorable patterns.

3. There are three main credit reporting agencies: Experian, Equifax, and TransUnion. Each of these agencies has access to your credit report and score.

If you have been diligently paying off your loans, you may still fall into the "high-risk" category if you have made late payments on all of your credit accounts (but not on time). This may seem picky, but banks can afford to be strict because there are so many people reapplying for credit.

4. Damage Control

If your credit rating allows it, consolidate all your consumer debts into one larger loan with a lower interest rate. This will accelerate the process of debt repayment by reducing the impact of interest on your payments, and it will help your credit score in the long run.

If your credit is good enough, you may be eligible for a balance transfer offer from one of your credit cards. This could help you pay off your debt more quickly by shifting your high-interest balances to a credit card account with a 0% APR and a grace period of six to eighteen months before you have to make a payment. Keep in mind that if you don't pay off your credit card balance by the end of the grace period, you will be subject to high interest rates. The only upfront cost will be a balance transfer fee, which can be either a flat fee or a percentage of the amount transferred (typically 3% to 5%).

Financial Aid

If you have access to a line of credit, such as a home-equity line of credit, you may be able to use the funds to pay down other, higher-interest debt, such as a credit card. Lines of credit often have APRs in the mid-single digits, while credit card APRs typically run from 10% to 20%.

Careful thought should be given before using a credit line to cover up bad spending habits or to live beyond one's means.

Closing a credit card or two may seem like a good idea because you won't be tempted to use them, but doing so can have a negative effect on your credit score, so keep them open and just put them away.

5. Use a pair of shovels

Although increasing the frequency of payments is not as successful as consolidation, it can shorten the payback period. It is recommended that payments be doubled on the debt with the highest interest rate whenever possible. This strategy is known as a "debt avalanche."

If you double your payments after getting a consolidation loan, you'll pay it off faster and get closer to the rate the bank wants to see before giving you a consolidation loan.

6. I Am Responsible, And I Will Carry Out My Duties.

If you're too far behind, drastic measures may be required. The easiest cuts are substitutions, such as using one-ply toilet paper instead of two, going for a walk in the park instead of joining a gym, or taking a "staycation" instead of going on a real vacation.

The most drastic measure is to sell any unnecessary possessions so the money can be put toward paying off the loan with the highest interest rate.

7. The Efforts of a Group Are Reduced When Individuals Contribute

To avoid getting to the point where you have no choice but to seek help from a credit counselor, it is recommended that you schedule an appointment with one before you reach financial crisis proportions.

Be wary of credit specialists that charge exorbitant fees and have a high customer volume, though; they may also be able to help you when you meet with your creditors, providing legitimacy to any discussions you want to conduct.

8. Discuss Renegotiating Terms

Now is the time to meet with your creditors; if you are working with a credit counselor, make sure you have thoroughly prepared and brought all relevant paperwork.

In order to avoid defaulting on your debts, you should get in touch with the financial institutions you owe money to. If you owe money to more than one bank, give the bank with which you have the best relationship the highest priority. Set up a meeting, and be sure to bring your damage report, your new cash-based budget, and a smile.

Now that you've shown that you've changed your bad credit habits for the better, banks will treat you more favorably. Now is also the time to seek the help of a debt relief or settlement company.

How Can You Eliminate Debt and Save Money at the Same Time?

Yes. You can eliminate debt and save money simultaneously, but it requires planning. Prioritize the debt with the highest rate of interest and always pay the minimum balance on your credit cards and loans. Plan to save aside a little portion of your income for retirement while you pay off your debts. Over time, even a small amount in a savings or money market account will grow.

As a second way to get rid of student debt or any other kind of debt, you could get a job that pays more and put more money toward paying it off.

How Can You Eradicate Your Real Estate Debt?

Mortgage debt in the United States is expected to reach trillions of dollars by 2020.6 If your mortgage debt is too high, you can take a few steps to reduce it. First, if your credit score is sufficient, inquire with your mortgage lender about refinancing for a reduced interest rate. Consequently, you may be able to reduce your payments. Making extra principal payments on your mortgage loan is a further method for eliminating mortgage debt. By doing so, you will reduce the total mortgage amount.

If you are unable to pay your mortgage, you should contact your mortgage lender immediately. Request the establishment of a payment plan or a loan modification. If market conditions are favorable, you can consider selling your home and settling your obligations. Obviously, you will need to plan for new housing if you choose this.

How Can You Get Out of Student Loan Debt?

There are numerous methods for paying off student loan debt. If you have multiple student loans, you may wish to consolidate them into a single loan with a lower interest rate. Look into loan forgiveness programs, which are usually only available for federal student loans or plans that are based on your income.

If your student loans are held privately, contact your lenders to see if you can negotiate a temporary payment plan with a lower amount of money.

There are five ways on this list that I have been making money for the last 10 years. I tried a few legit ways earlier, but now I am not working because of the time constraint.

And finally, there are some ways I never tried, but I know these are the best ways, and thousands of people are making money online from these methods.

1. Earn Money Through Blogging

I have been earning money by blogging for almost 11 years. I have made more than 2 million dollars from blogging.

But I was a little confused when I started my career in blogging.

I had zero ideas about blogging when I started my first blog in 2009. I worked very hard for this blog but made no money for almost one year.

But I did not give up! I researched topics on Google like:

- **How to create a blog**
- **How to Write Content**

- How to promote your blog on the internet.
- How to make money from your blog

During those 12 months, I learned a lot about blogging.

And things were starting to move in my favor after some time. I made my first $100+ (from Google AdSense) from blogging in 2011. Then there was no looking back. Today, I make almost $25,000 (Rs 15 lacs+) monthly from blogging.

More about my blogging journey, income proofs, and a complete guide to starting a blog are available for FREE.

2. Start a YouTube channel

YouTube is the hot craze in 2022. Everyone wants to become a YouTuber. Everyone wants to make a lot of money and fame through YouTube.

If you want high motivation, you can see the list of these famous and highest subscribed YouTubers here on SureJob who are making millions from YouTube.

You don't need to live your job, studies, or other things to be a YouTuber. You can even do it part-time and make sufficient money.

Here are the exact steps if you want to be a successful YouTuber:

Step 1: Pick a niche.

You need to decide the topics you want to choose for your videos. I create videos on digital marketing on my channel, Pritam Nagrale.

You can choose a niche like comedy videos, motivation, self-help, vlogs, interview series, kitchen recipes, health, how-to-do videos, travel tips, news channels, sports, gaming, or similar on YouTube.

Step 2: Make a Channel

Create a YouTube channel in your name. Add an attractive profile pic and a banner image. Edit your bio section and include some quality information about yourself, as I have done on my Pritam Nagrale channel.

Step 3: Produce videos

It's best if you have a professional camera, but you can also use your smartphone camera. Check for a proper quiet place and suitable lights to shoot good quality videos.

Step 4: Spread the word about your videos.

Though YouTube tries to promote your videos, you can get views and subscribers fast if you put some effort into it. You can start promoting it by sending it to your friends and list on social platforms like WhatsApp, Facebook, Instagram, etc.

A good title, description, and thumbnail will also help you get more views on your videos.

Step 5: Make money from your videos.

Once your channel reaches 1000 subscribers and 4000 hours of video views within 12 months, you can apply for the YouTube partner program. YouTube plays ads in your videos and pays you for the number of views your video receives.

Once you reach 5000 or 10,000 subscribers, companies will approach you for sponsorship.

For sponsoring one video, they pay Rs. 5000 to Rs. 10,000 to micro publishers and more than a

lac to mega influencers.I have sponsored videos for my channel, Pritam Nagrale and DMatic Digital.

3. Affiliate Marketing

Affiliate marketing was an excellent way to earn money online in 2004 when I started my online career with affiliate marketing. It is still the most lucrative business on the internet.

Affiliate marketing promotes and sells products of online companies like Amazon, eBay, Clickbank, and thousands of others. You can find a list of the 99 best affiliate programs available in India here.

I use various channels to promote my affiliate products, such as my blogs, SureJob and MoneyConnexxion, YouTube channels, email list, and other micro-affiliate sites.

I even use paid marketing like Google Ads and Native Ads to promote some profitable affiliate programs that pay $50+ for each sale or lead.

There are other ways as well that you can use to promote affiliate programs, like Pinterest, Quora, Medium, Instagram, etc.

Thousands of affiliates make $5000+ every month promoting different affiliate programs and networks like Amazon, CJ, ShareASale, Clickbank, finance and crypto affiliate programs, and various others.

4. Work as a Freelancer

Freelancing is a great work from home option in which you work independently for your clients on short-term contracts.Sometimes it can be permanent, depending on the mutual understanding.

Here, basically, you sell your skills to your clients. You must have expertise in some field before you work as a freelancer. You can provide freelancing services in content writing, digital marketing, graphic designing, app development, or any other area.

Most freelancers earn between $1000 to $5000 per month depending on various factors like freelance work, client budget, the number of hours daily, etc.

There are 25–30 popular freelance sites like People Per Hour, UpWork, Fiverr, WorkNHire, etc. You can get many clients from these platforms.

But there is a lot of competition on these platforms. You need to create an attractive profile, provide your services for reasonable rates, and collect some good reviews from clients before you charge high rates to your clients.

5. Make Money Through Online Surveys

Do you know that you can earn money by taking online surveys? Depending on the length of the surveys, it takes 5 minutes to 10 minutes and sometimes 30 minutes to complete a survey.

There are various market research companies where you can become a member if you want to make money using this method.

These companies send you simple online surveys where they ask for your feedback on some products or services. Your feedback helps these companies to create excellent products.

It's very easy to take an online survey because they just give you multiple choices and you need to select your answer. There is nothing wrong or right with your answers because it's your opinion.

You can earn $1 to $20 for taking each survey. You need to provide as much detail as you can in your profile so that companies will learn more about you and send you more surveys that match your profile.

You can find more about paid online surveys and a list of the best survey sites here.

6. Work as a Captcha Solver

Do you have some free time, like 1-2 hours daily? If so, then you can make additional cash by working as a captcha solver.

Captcha solving jobs are one of the easiest ways to earn money online. Here you need to read the captcha images and type exactly the same characters through the software.

You can get paid $2 to $3 for every 1000 captchas you solve from these sites. If your typing is good, you can solve more captchas every hour.

.

7. Work as a Virtual Assistant to Earn Money

A VA (virtual assistant) acts as a personal assistant for her clients. Clients may be temporary or permanent. You need to take the instructions from your clients and work accordingly.

You don't need to be physically present for this online job.

You can do a variety of tasks for your clients, like accounting, writing & proofreading, publishing content, maintaining websites or apps, digital marketing, coding, website and app development, research, data entry, etc.

Some of the companies like MyTasker, uAssistMe, HireMyMom, 123Employee, etc. provide VA jobs. Just sign up on these websites and create an attractive profile.

You can definitely get 1 to 2 projects in the next 30 days.

8. Job in Writing

Writing is another excellent and popular way to earn money online. Here you can get paid to write various types of content.

You can write articles for blogs, create content for social media pages, copy, scripts, books, etc., for companies, institutions, individual people, etc.

Most writers earn $10 to $50 for creating 1,000 words of content. You must have good experience in content writing before you charge a high amount for writing.

If you think that you can't make money with writing jobs because you don't have writing skills, you are wrong.

It's easy to get this skill and become a writer. Read this post to learn how to become an expert in content writing.

There are various platforms like UpWork, iWriter, WriterBay, FreelanceWriting,

and TextBroker to find content writing jobs and writing assignments.

9. Microjobs

If you are looking for an easier option, then micro-jobs may be another opportunity for you. You can easily earn $200 to $300 every month by doing simple online tasks on different sites.

Signing up on a website, downloading an app, watching a video, identifying an object, checking ad ratings and finding contact information, doing some research, writing 100-200 word articles, and so on.

There are a few websites like Amazon Mechanical Turk, MicroWorker, SEOClerk, etc. where you can sign up as a micro-job worker. You can earn some additional income from these websites.

10. Online Sales

Last year, I published an interview video (which went viral) of an online seller, Mr. Nimit Lodha, on my channel Pritam Nagrale. Mr. Nimit is an

Amazon and Flipkart seller with a Rs. 50 crore annual revenue.

That is the power of online selling.

Online selling is very much different than traditional selling. In the traditional way, there is not much scope for selling your products or services outside your local area, but in online selling, you can sell your products and services all over the country and even globally.

Here are the two best ways to sell your products online.

The first way is to create an e-commerce website for your business and sell your products from your online store. Second, you can become a seller with Amazon, Flipkart, or other top online shopping sites.

The second option is much better and more simple. You don't need to hunt for customers. You can get millions of existing customers from these reputed online stores.

Are you thinking,thinking, what if I don't have any products?

Many Amazon and Flipkart sellers don't own any productsproducts, but theyare still are still selling various products on these platforms and making a profit from this business.

What you can do is go to your local market andand try to find some exclusive products that you can sell on Amazon or Flipkart. For exampleFor example, if you go to the Manish Market in Mumbai, you can findmany of the many of the best products at a much cheaper ratethan on than on Amazon.

Another option is to import cheap products from other neighboring countries.

There is a lot of competition on Amazon and other shopping portals. You need to strike a balance between your price and profit margin to become a successful seller.

11. Domain Investing

Domain trading is one of the most profitable businessesbusinesses if you have good research skills in buying domain names that may fetch an excellent amount in the future but are still available to grab.

Last year, I was doing casual research for domain name availability, and I found a good name. Though I don't deal in domain trading, I booked it.

A few days later, I got a message from someone asking me to sell this domain name. I had no experience with this, so I started the conversation.

At first, he offered me $500, but I said no. He then sent me an email asking how much I was willing to sell it for.At first, he offered me $500, but I said no. He then sent me an email asking how much I was willing to sell it for .At first, he offered me $500, but I said no. He then sent me an email asking how much I was willing to sell it for.

I asked him for $4000, but after some negotiation, I sold the domain for $2000.

I bought it for just $17 and sold it for $2000—almost 115 times profit.

That is why domain traders make thousands of dollars selling domain names every month. That is why domain traders make thousands of dollars selling domain names every month. That is why

domain traders make thousands of dollars selling domain names every month.

If you actively search for quality domains and buy them buy them buy them, you can sell them for aaa very high amount to companies in the future.

When a company finds that the domain name they are name they are looking for is available with you, they will send you a message to buy it. Now you need to set the price according to the demand and negotiate with the company, as I did in my case.

.

12. Flipping Websites

Website flipping is also a good way to earn money online. It's similar to domain trading, but here with websites.

That means here, you have to buy a website and sell it for a higher price in the future. There are various platforms, like Flippa Empire Flippers, which you can use for website flipping.

You will find thousands of buyers on these platforms who are interested in buying your website for 40 times to 50 times the price of your average monthly profit.

For example, if you make a net profit of $500 from AdSense or affiliate programs or both from your website, you can sell it for $20,000 to $25,000.

There are two ways to sell a website on these platforms.

The first is to start a new blog, work on it for 6 months to a year, monetize it with AdSense and affiliate programs for the next 3 to 4 months, and sell it.

The second way is to buy an existing website with some traffic and revenue from Flippa, work on it for the next 3 to 6 months, grow the profit, and sell it again on Flippa.

This is a much better way to go , as it's easier to grow the profit of an existing website with traffic as compared to a new website.

Many experienced flippers purchase such profitable websites from Flippa or other

marketplaces and make a huge profit by selling them again.

13. Provide training and consulting services

Do you have some skills that people need badly? You might know a lot about the stock market, some subjects, meditation, motivation, money management, nutrition, starting your own business, etc. You might know a lot about the stock market, some subjects, meditation, motivation, money management, nutrition, starting your own business, etc. You might know a lot about the stock market, some subjects, meditation, motivation, money management, nutrition, starting your own business, etc.

There is a tremendous scope if you create training or a course around your skill and sell it online. People are earning thousands selling these courses through Facebook or Instagram.

You can create a landing page for your business where you can describe your product and how it can benefit people who buy it.

Just drive traffic from Facebook or Instagram to your product page and sell it in India and other countries.

You can also get free traffic from YouTube, Google search, and a variety of social media platforms. You can also get free traffic from YouTube, Google search, and a variety of social media platforms. You can also get free traffic from YouTube, Google search, and a variety of social media platforms.

14. Trading in stocks and forex

Stock trading and forex trading some two other profitable ways to earn money. But if you are just a beginner, I would recommend you get some basic training in this before you invest your money.

Several free and paid training courses are available on Google and YouTube to get training in the stock market. You should be careful before buying any course because there are so-called gurus who have not made a single penny, but they claim to be millionaires You can even begin reading newspapers such as the Economic Times

or watching TV channels such as CNBC, forex, cryptos , or NFTs without enough knowledge.

15. Make money using your smartphone

There are many money-making apps available in thein the in the Google Play store and iOS store that

CHAPTER FIVE

INVEST AS A STRANGER

(RETIREMENT AND WEALTH)

Capital allocation can be defined as the process of deciding how to deploy a firm's resources to earn the best possible return for shareholders. Understanding and evaluating a company's capital allocation decisions, process, and history is therefore critical to analysing potential investments.

One of my favourite books on capital allocation is The Outsiders. This book was written by William Thorndike,Thorndike,Thorndike, who reflected that "*Surprisingly, in business the best are not studied as closely as in other fields like medicine, the law, politics, politics ,politics, or sports,*" and "*Despite its importance, there are no courses on capital allocation at the top business schools.*"

Includes focuses focuses book focusses on eight 'companies' share prices massively outperformed the market. The list of CEO's includes Henry

Singleton from Teledyne, John Malone from Liberty Media, Katherine Graham from the Washington Post, Tom Murphy from Capital Cities Broadcasting, and, of course, Warren Buffett fact, ,of Berkshire Hathaway. In fact, the book was the number one book on Mr. Buffett's recommended reading list. Mr. in 2012. Mr. Thorndike noted these CEOs "*thought more like investors than managers*." It's that surprise that surprise that many of the characteristics that define great company managers are common to the Investment Masters.

Effective capital allocation......... requires a certain temperament. To be successful, , you have to think like an investor, dispassionately and probabilistically, with a certain coolness. " coolness. " coolness. " Michael Maboussin

While each of the Outsider CEOs were intensities—there intensities—there operated in different industries—some industries——some growing while others declining, with different capital intensities—there were many commonalities in how they managed their businesses. While it wasn't rocket science, the

management style and initiatives these eight CEOs implemented were <u>unconventional</u> for the time.

Some of the common characteristics include :

Acquisitions: While most of the CEOs were involved in acquisitions , they were both opportunistic and <u>patient</u> were Acquisitions were only made when there were compelling discrepancies between value and <u>price</u> or when significant cost savings could be extracted. These CEOs either refrained from or were reluctant to issue stock for acquisitions , and only if the scrip was expensive and the "business value" [i.e. intrinsic value] acquired was greater than the "business " value""" given.

This latter point, in my view, is one of the most common mistakes CEOs and company boards make. They acquire expensive assets funded via either scrip mergers or capital raisings when their own share prices do not reflect their company's worth. While acquired assets may be high quality and accr-tive to earnings, these acquisitions can be hugely value-destroying

Warren Buffett gave a great overview of this common situation in his 1982 annual Berkshire letter. Warren Buffett gave a great overview of

this common situation in his 1982 annual Berkshire letter .Warren Buffett gave a great overview of this common situation in his 1982 annual Berkshire letter.

Our share issuances follow a simple basic rule; we will not issue shares unless we receive as much intrinsic business value as we give. Such a policy might seem axiomatic. Why, you might ask, would anyone issue dollar bills in exchange for fifty-cent pieces? Unfortunately, many corporate managers have been willing to do just. " that. "

"[In relation to] the acquirer who ends up using an undervalued (market value) currency to pay for a fully valued (negotiated value) property. In effect, the acquirer must give up $2 of value to receive $1 of value. Under such circumstances, a marvellous business purchased at a fair sales price becomes a terrible buy. For gold worth its weight in gold can't be bought smartly with gold or even silver worth its weight in lead ."Warren Buffett

Outsider CEOs were not in the business of growing for the sake of growing. If another party wanted to pay an inflated price for an asset and the CEO no longer saw the growth potential of that asset, they would not be afraid to shrink the business, sometimes substantially. If the market was undervaluing a part of the business, the CEO

would look to spin-off the division to realise that value. Should a business be underperforming with little prospect of a turnaround, , it is likely slated for sale or closed. The Outsider CEOs were not emotionally attached to any division, , and they cut their losing businesses long-term. Capital investment was reserved only for those businesses with attractive returns on capital. The core focus was on was on maximising long-term value per share, not organisational size or growth.

***Buy-backs::: the CEOs were opportunistic acquirers of their own shares, but only when they deemed them to be trading below "business value." In many cases, shares were repurchased in bear markets or when P/E's were at cyclical lows. Sometimes these buybacks area substantial. For example, in the case of Teledyne, over 90% of the shares are at are at issue. All potential acquisitions were compared with the returns available from buybacks. Once again, CEOs were not afraid to shrink their businesses.**

The CEOs focused on cash flow per share, , not reported net income. The Outsider CEOs believed the "*key to long-term value creation was to optimise free cash flow, and this emphasis on cash informed all aspects of how they ran their companies-from companies from the way they paid*

for acquisitions and managed their balance sheets to their accounting policies and compensation systems."

***Humility—the Outsider CEOs were humble, understated, and analytical. The Outsider CEOs were distinctly "*unpromotional. Mr.*". Thorndike noted they "*had familiarity with other companies and industries and disciplines, and this ranginess translated into new perspectives, which in turn helped them to develop new approaches that eventually translated into exceptional results.*"**

None of the outsider CEOs provided Wall Street with advice. Their focus was to increase to increase to increase the long-term value per share. Taking a longer term view realizing meant, at times, making investments or capital expenditures that may have detracted from short term earnings but added to long term value. The Outsider CEOs were frugal regards to dividends, realizing the compounding benefits of reinvesting capital either in the business or in their own shares should their prices be depressed.

***Decentralisation::: the CEOs ran decentralised organisations where significant autonomy was given to operating managers .This let managers at the front lines respond quickly to changes in the market, while CEOs could focus on allocating**

capital and making long-term plans. This let managers at the front lines respond quickly to changes in the market, while CEOs could focus on allocating capital and making long-term plans. This let managers at the front lines respond quickly to changes in the market, while CEOs could focus on allocating capital and making long-term plans.

Flexibility: the CEOs recognised the need to remain flexible as business conditions and markets were uncertain and constantly changing acquisitions, ,. At certain times, , it made sense to make acquisitions, while other times favoured selling or spinning off assets. The Outsider CEOs did not have an ideology and were not bound by a strategy.

CHAPTER SIX

LEARN HOW TO USE INSURANCE INCREASE YOUR WEALTH

{INCREASE YOUR NET WORTH}

What Does "Does "Does "Personal Insurance"Insurance"Insurance" Mean?

Personal insurance is any policy that isn't a business policy. You buy it to protect yourself from financial losses that you couldn't pay for on your own. It has to do with the risks you might face because of accidents, illnesses, death, or damage to your property.

What is the point of insurance?

You pay the company money when you buy insurance. In exchange for these payments, which are called "premiums," you are protected from certain risks. The company promises to pay you back if you lose money. Insurance is based on the idea that if many people share the risk of a loss, like a fire or a theft, the risk is lower for everyone. Many people buy insurance from the company. All of them pay a premium. Each client won't lose money at the same time. When something bad happens, they might get money from their insurance to pay for it.

You don't have to buy it, but it's a good idea if you have a lot of money on the line or investments that could go bad. But when a third party has a financial stake in the property, like when a bank has a mortgage on it, having insurance is usually a requirement for the loan to be approved.

Some types of insurance are optional, while others, like auto insurance, may have minimum requirements set by law.

Why does the bank insist that you have insurance?

Not all types of insurance are required by law. If you borrowed money from a lender, bank, or mortgage company to buy something like a house or car that cost a lot of money, they will want to see it.

If you take out a loan to buy a car or house, you will need insurance on it. If you have a car loan, you need car insurance, and if you have a home loan, you need home insurance. It is usually needed to get a loan for a big purchase like a house. Lenders want to make sure you are covered against risks that could lower the value of youryouryour car or home if you lose it before you pay it off. off. off. 1

How to Find Cheap Insurance

The premium is the amount of money an insurance company will charge you for the financial security your policy gives you. you. you. You can pay once a year, twice a year, or once a month. Shop around with different companies or use a broker who can do the shopping for you to lower your premium. Get at least three quotes from different companies to see which one can give you the best price. Rates will vary based on how claims are handled and how the insurance company writes policies. If you stop paying for your car or home insurance, your lender will buy their own and charge you for it. It's not a good idea to do this. The cost of lender insurance is higher than the cost of a policy you buy on your own.

Some businesses may offer discounts to attract t a certain type of customer. How good your rate is will depend on how well your profile matches the insurer's profile.

For example, if an insurance company wants to attract younger customers, it might develop programs that give discounts to recent college graduates or young families. Other insurers may come up with programs that give seniors and people in the military bigger discounts. You can't find out unless you look around, compare policies, and get quotes.

When is the right time to buy insurance?

You should buy it for three main reasons:

1. Like having liability insurance for your car, it is required by law.

2. It's needed by a lender, like when you buy a house and get a home policy.

3. A financial loss could be more than you can pay for or easily get back on your feet. For example, you should get renter's insurance if you have expensive computer equipment in your apartment.

What are the fivefivefive main kinds of personal insurance?

When most people think about personal insurance, they probably think of one of these five main types, among others:

1. Residential insurance, such as for a house, condo, or co-op, or insurance for renters,,,

2. Car insurance and insurance for other vehicles, like motorcycles, are also available.

3. Boat insurance, which is sometimes covered by home insurance, and separate boat insurance for boats that are too fast or too long to be covered by home insurance.

4. **There is life and disability insurance, as well as health insurance.**

5. **Liability insurance, which can be in any of these groups, , , It protects you from being sued if you cause someone else to lose something and you are to blame.**
6.

You might be able to get some of your policies from the same company, but this isn't always the case. Insurance is broken up into groups and requires a license. This means that someone must have a license from the state to sell and give advice on the type you are buying before they are legally allowed to do so.

For example, your home insurance broker or agent may tell you that they don't offer life or disability insurance. They might be able to put you in touch with a licensed agent in their circle who can sell you a policy.

If you can buy more than one type of policy from the same person, you may be able to "bundle" your insurance and get a discount for doing so.

What does a policy for a home cover?

The buildings on your property are covered by your homeowner's insurance. This includes your main home and any other buildings on the property. It also covers the things inside your home;;; the things you keep at home that you can move;;; living expenses if you have to leave your home because of a loss;;; and liability.

Renters' Insurance covers the things you keep in your rental unit as well as the cost of living elsewhere if something happens to your home. It also covers your personal liability at home and anywhere else in the world.

The insurance for a condo or co-op is like renters' Insurance. In addition to your personal property, living expenses, and liability, it covers

some things that are unique to owning a unit or share in a building.

You should always read the fine print of your insurance policy because not all policies are the same.

Insurance for your car, boat, and any other vehicle.

Car, boat, and other vehicle insurance can cover a lot of different things. Liability insurance is the most important. This protects you from legal trouble if you own or drive the car or boat. You can also buy extra coverage such as ones that cover damage to the vehicle or boat itself or to its parts. Medical payments to others and death benefits if someone dies or gets hurt because of how the car is driven may also be extra or required, depending on the state's laws on financial responsibility or minimum car insurance requirements.

Insurance For health care, life, and disability

Health, life, disability, and other less common types of insurance, like long-term care, all offer coverage that will pay you if something bad happens to your health, makes you sick, or kills you.

There are many different kinds of health insurance policies. You can get basic health benefits as well as dental or long-term care policies. You can find many different kinds of insurance to meet your needs.

7 Insurance Terms You Should Know

In the fine print of your policy, you will find these key phrases. It helps to understand what they say.

1. When you file a claim, you will pay the amount of your deductible. When your deductible is higher, you take on more risk, but your payments will be lower. Some people choose a high deductible to save money on their insurance premiums.

2. Your policy doesn't cover things that aren't in it. Ask about the exclusions before you buy a

policy so that the fine print doesn't catch you off guard when you need to make a claim.

3. Different types of policies are available from different companies. If you get a quote for a really low price, you should ask what kind of policy it is and what its limits are. Compare these details to what you know from other quotes.

4. Each policy has a section with a list of the maximummaximummaximum it will pay out. This is true for all types of insurance, from health to auto. When you are making a claim, this is very important. Ask what kinds of coverage are limited and how much they cover. If the limits shown on the policy worry you, you can usually ask for a different type of policy that gives you higher limits.

5. Waiting Periods and Special Clauses: Before you are covered by some types of insurance, you have to wait a certain amount of time. For example, you may have to wait for dental care. A contestability period may apply to you if you have life insurance. These are only a couple of examples. You should always inquire as to when your coverage will begin.You should always inquire as to when your coverage will begin.You should always inquire as to when your coverage will begin.When you buy a new policy, you

should also ask if there are any waiting periods or special clauses that could change what you're covered for.

6. Add-ons to a policy that give you more coverage are called endorsements. In some cases, they may change a policy so that it covers less or less.

7. The terms of how the claim will be paid are shown in the Basis of Claims Settlement. You could get a replacement cost or actual cash value policy for your home insurance, for example. How claims are settled has a big effect on how much money you get. You should always find out how claims are paid and how they will be handled.

How do insurance companies pay out claims?

When you have a loss, like a car accident or house fire, you will call your insurance company right away to let them know. They will write down your claim and look into it to find out what happened and how you are covered. Once they decide that your loss is covered, they may send you a check or, if you were in a car accident, they may send a check to the shop where your car was

fixed. The check will cover your loss, less the amount of your deductible. You will have to pay for that yourself.

If you don't make a claim, do you get your money back?

When you've been paying for insurance for a long time, you may start to wonder why you're paying so much if you've never had to use it. Some people may even think they should get their money back when they haven't made a claim. It doesn't work like that. Insurance companies take your moey and put it away so that they can pay out claims when they come up.

This is what "shared risk" means. The idea is that over time, the amount paid out in claims will be less than the amount paid in premiums. You might feel like you're throwing money out the window if you never file a claim, but knowing that you're covered in case of a big loss can be worth its weight in gold.

Premiums vs. Claims Payments

Take a look at this example to see how premium payments and claims payments are different.

Let's say you pay $500 a year to cover your $200,000 home with insurance. You've been paying for 10 years and haven't made a claim. That's $500 a year for 10 years. This means that you've paid $5,000 for home insurance. You start to wonder why you're paying so much for nothing. In the 11th year, your kitchen has a fire that needs to be fixed. The business gives you $50,000 to fix up your kitchen.

If the insurance company gave back everyone's money when there was no claim, they would never have enough money to pay out when there was a claim. Even though you paid them $5,000 over 10 years, that doesn't make up for the $50,000 you lost. If you have even one loss, the company can no longer make money off of you. Because insurance is based on spreading risk among many people, it is the money that everyone pays that allows the company to build assets and pay claims when they happen.

What makes rates go up or down for insurance?

A business is insurance. Even though it would be nice for the companies to keep rates the same all the time, they have to make enough money to pay for all the claims their policyholders might make.

When a company compares how much they paid out in claims to how much they got in premiums at the end of the year, they have to change their rates to make money. Changes to underwriting and increases or decreases in rates are based on how well the insurance company did in the past.

Depending on which company you buy it from, you may be dealing with a captive agent. They only sell policies from one company. A broker works with many different insurance companies.

Agents, Captive Agents, and Insurance Brokers: What Are They?

When you buy insurance, the agents and brokers who work for the insurance company are the first

people you talk to. They will talk about the kinds of goods they sell.

The captive agent works for one insurance company only. They know about the products or servicesthat athat a that a company offers, but they can't talk about other companies' policies, prices, or products.

A broker or independent agent can work on your behalf with more than one insurance company. They will be able to work with more than one company, and they must know what kinds of products each company sells.

How to Choose the Right Coverage

You can decide what kind of coverage you need by asking yourself a few important questions.

- How much money loss or risk are you willing to take on your own?

- **If you have an accident, do you have enough money to pay for your bills and costs? What if your house or car gets destroyed?**

- **Do you have enough money saved in case you get sick or hurt and can't work?**

- **Can you afford higher deductibles in order to save money?Can you afford higher deductibles in order to save money?Can you afford higher deductibles in order to save money?**

- **Do you need extra coverage because you have special needs?**

- **What do you worry about most? Policies can be made to fit your needs and protect the things you care most about. This could help you figure out what kind of insurance you need and cut your costs.**

Choosing a policy based on how you live now and where you are in life

What kind of insurance you need depends on where you are in life, what assets you own, and what your long-term goals and responsibilities are. That's why it's important to talk to your agent about what you want from your policy. Getting the right insurance is a good way to keep track of your money. Even if you have a covered loss, it will help you keep your money safe.

How does insurance from the FDIC work?

The Federal Deposit Insurance Corporation (FDIC) was set up by the government in 1933 to help make the financial system stronger. If a bank fails, FDIC insurance will pay back deposits. No matter what happens to the bank, if you bank with an FDIC-insured institution, your money is safe (up to $250,000 per depositor per institution). institution). institution). 3

How does gap insurance work?

Guaranteed auto protection (also called "gap") insurance is a type of car insurance for people who bought their car with a loan. Gap insurance will pay off the part of your loan that standard auto insurance doesn't cover if you take out a loan to buy a car and something happens to it. Some lenders insist that their borrowers have gap insurance.

Using Your Health Insurance

It's important to have health insurance, but it's not always easy to understand. You might have to do a few things to make sure that your health insurance will pay for your medical bills. There are also a lot of important words and phrases to remember. Here are some basics you should know:

CHAPTER SEVEN

PICK YOUR FINANCIAL TEAM

(FINANCIAL PROFESSIONALS).

How to Put Together Your Best Financial Team

Yes, you may need to hire a financial expert – or even four of them – to save your money.

Your team of financial superheroes should include different types of experts who can help you set financial goals, save money on taxes, and write up legal documents. Who you choose to work with will depend on how old you are, what your goals are, and how complicated your financial situation is. "The more money you have, the more people you usually need on your team," says Kelly Graves, a certified financial planner

and partner at Charlotte, North Carolina's Carroll Financial Associates.

Here is a list of all the experts you might want to add to your financial "dream team."

Planner for money. A financial planner is like a team captain for your money. This expert can look at your financial statements, help you set goals, and answer your questions. As team captain, he or she will also work with the rest of your financial team to make sure everything runs smoothly. He or she will share regular reports and give you advice on how to talk to legal and tax experts.

Financial advisor who is a certified financial planner and will act as a fiduciary, which means they will give you advice that is in your best interest and not based on how much money they can make from you. You can find financial planners in your area in a number of ways. The National Association of Personal Financial Advisors is a group of financial advisors who only work for a fee. You can look through their database. Or you can check out the Financial

Planning Association, which has the most certified financial planner members. Think about a financial expert from the Garrett Planning Network. Members of this group offer advice for an hourly fee.

How much it costs to hire a financial planner depends on how much they charge, where they are located, and what services they offer. You could pay $150 or more per hour, or 0.5 to 1.5 percent of your assets' value. You could pay $150 or more per hour, or 0.5 to 1.5 percent of your assets' value. You could pay $150 or more per hour, or 0.5 to 1.5 percent of your assets' value. Don't be afraid to ask about this fee right away when you talk to potential planners.

See how to these understand these 10 confusing financial terms confusing financial terms.

*Help with taxes. If your tax situation is more complicated than what your online tax software can handle, you may want to add a tax professional to your financial A-team.

If you already have a financial advisor you like, ask him or her for a recommendation. Experts say it's important for your pros to talk to each other and work well together. Consider looking for a "certified public accountant." This means that the person is a qualified accountant who has passed tests and gotten a license. The title "enrolled agent" is given to a tax expert who has shown the Internal Revenue Service that they know a lot about taxes and who specializes in taxes. The National Association of Enrolled Agents can help you find one.

The cost will depend on a number of things, such as how complicated your tax situation is. Allan Katz, president of Comprehensive Wealth Management Group in Staten Island, New York, says, "The more complicated it is, the more it will cost." "It costs between $150 and $300 per hour, depending on what you need."

***Lawyer for estate planning. Depending on your age and family situation, you may want to hire an estate planning attorney to help you make important legal documents like a will, advance health care directive, and durable power of attorney.**

Experts say to find a lawyer who specializes in this kind of planning for the end of life. As Graves As says, "I feel very strongly that you don't hire the same person to handle your family's traffic ticket this month and your estate next month."

The amount you'll pay varies. Common legal documents can be written by an attorney for a flat fee of several hundred dollars. You could also pay by the hour. People in the Providence, Rhode Island, area pay between $2,500 and $4,000, says Jason Archambault, managing member of SK Wealth Management in Providence, for more advanced estate planning, depending on the law firm.

The good news is that you don't have to meet with this professional as often as you might think. A financial planner can tell you when you need to talk to your estate attorney and update your plan because your life has changed or the law has changed. One that's good might even be able

***Agents for insurance. Make sure you have the right insurance for your needs to cover you in case of an emergency. Your financial planner can help you figure out what kind of coverage you need and how much of it you need. He or she can also suggest an insurance agent. When you and your financial advisor decide ahead of time what kindkindkind and how much of each insurance product you need, you can avoid being sold too many products you don't need.**

***In an email, James In an email, James Dew, a certified financial planner and president and CEO of Dew Wealth Management in Scottsdale, Arizona, says in an email that you can also check with your state's insurance department to find out how long someone has been licensed. "You don't want to pay for someone to learn," he says.**

Depending on your financial situation, you may also want to look into a certified private wealth advisor, a private banker who can help you get a bridge loan, and an investment advisor. No matter who you hire for your financial A-team, Katz says, "Make sure that all of these professionals can talk to each other and work well together."

As I have written before, the ecosystem of financial advisors can be surprisingly complicated. With only a few qualifications, almost anyone can call themselves a financial advisor, financial planner, or financial coach. So, it's important to be careful and thoughtful when choosing a professional to help you save, grow, and protect your savings.

When looking for a financial advisor, here are five things to think about.

Education and Work History

Check out your potential advisor's education and experience to find out why he or she might be the best person to help you with your finances. In particular, look for advisors who have shown they can use their knowledge to come up with the best plan for you.

The advisor's website and articles could be a good place to start if you want to learn about their background, how they plan, and how they think. You can find out a lot about independent advisors who are registered in their states or with the U.S. Broker Check is a free tool from FINRA that lets you look up information about advisors who work for a brokerage firm as well as the Securities and Exchange Commission (SEC).

Certifications

Try to figure out what steps a financial advisor has taken to keep learning more about personal finance. One way to figure this out is to look at the certifications they have. In particular, take the time to learn about both the initial steps you need to take to get a certificate and the ongoing steps you need to take to keep it.

For example, in the field of financial planning, the Certified Financial Planner (CFP®) designation is seen as the gold standard. For planners to get the CFP® designation, they have to take a lot of specialized classes, pass a six-hour exam, and have three years of experience in the field. Certified people have to do at least 30 hours of continuing education every two years.

Other common designations include Certified Public Accountant (CPA) and Enrolled Agent (EA) for planners who may specialize in accounting and taxes, Chartered Financial Analyst (CFA) for advisors who focus on portfolio management and investing, and Accredited Financial Counselor (AFCAFCAFC) for advisors who may focus on coaching and counseling.

Fees and Personal Interests

Learn more aboutLearn more aboutLearn more about how a financial advisor is paid to learn more about their possible incentives and conflicts of interest. Most advisors get paid through 1) client fees ("fee-only"), 2) commissions, or 3) a combination of both ("fee-based").

Julie Ford, a CFP and financial planner at Ford Financial Solutions, says, "When you work with someone who calls themselves a financial advisor, make sure you know how they are getting paid for the service they are providing. When commissions are involved, it becomes harder for the advisor to stay independent and put your interests ahead of theirown. "own. " own. "

Even if they say they aren't, advisors are always influenced by how they get paid, says Justin Chidester, AFC®, a financial planner at Wealth Mode Financial Planning. "This could be on purpose or by accident."

Most of the time, advisors use at least one of the following pricing models:

1.

Hourly Rate: Determined by the length of time they work with you.Hourly Rate: Determined by the length of time they work with you.Hourly

Rate: Determined by the length of time they work with you.

2.

Fixed or Flat or Fixed or Flat Fee: Based on a flat fee that was agreed upon.

3.

Assets Under Management Fee: Based on a percentage of the assets they manage for you.

Lori Dietzler, a CFP and financial planner at Zero Gravity Financial, recommends that people find a financial planner who charges a flat fee. This is true for all of the fee models.

Over the past ten years, the industry has moved away from commission-based pay to asset-based fees. This change has removed the financial incentive to actively trade client portfolios and/or invest in funds with high front-end or back-end expenses, " " "Dietzler says. Financial advisors also know from experience that it doesn't cost a firm more to manage a portfolio of $5 million

than a portfolio of $1 million. So why should clients pay more in fees for the same services? Flat fees align services with a fair price model used by other professionals, like accountants, lawyers, and doctors.

Be sure to look for and think about any fees that come with the investments that are being recommended.

David Oransky, a CFP® and financial planner at Laminar Wealth, suggests that you not only pay attention to how the advisor is paid but also to the total costcostcost of their strategy, such as fees, taxes, and trading costs.

According to a study done by Personal Capital, the average Merrill Lynch advisory fee is 1.30 percent, but the total fee is almost 2 percent because the investments themselves charge an extra 0.70 percent.

4.

Care Standard

Registered investment advisory firms (RIAsRIAsRIAs) must be fiduciaries, which means they must always put their clients' best interests ahead of everything else.

On the other hand, bank and brokerage advisors may only have to meet a suitability standard for now. With a suitability standard, a recommendation doesn't have to be the best for you; it just has to be the right one for you.

But Oransky says, "With the upcoming DOL fiduciary regulations, many advisors will suddenly claim fiduciary status. While this will be true in some parts of client relationships, it won't be everywhere, so buyer beware. The highest standard of care, and what every client should demand, is an advisor who acts as a fiduciary in all parts of the client relationship, at all times, and on all accounts.

Chidester suggests asking advisors, "What topics, decisions, or parts of your advice don't hold you to a fiduciary standard?"

Relationships at Work

Before you join, make sure you know how often and with whom you'll be talking. Some advisors have an initial meeting with clients and then check in with them once a year.Other advisors help with putting plans into action and working with other service providers, like insurance agents, mortgage brokers, and accountants, all year long.Other advisors help with putting plans into action and working with other service providers, like insurance agents, mortgage brokers, and accountants, all year long. Other advisors help with putting plans into action and working with other service providers, like insurance agents, mortgage brokers, and accountants, all year long.

Transparency is just as important as meeting the schedule and level of service. "Ask yourself, 'Does the advisor make it seem like my situation is so complicated that I could never handle it on

my own?'" says Jamie Menges, CFP®, a principal and client advisor at PDS Planning. "Does the advisor make it seem like my situation is so complicated that I could never handle it on my own?" I want an advisor who tells me that I might be able to handle my own planning at some point. Most clients don't have such complicated situations that they couldn't do it on their own if they wantedto. "to. " to. "

Hard work pays off.

At the end of the day, not every financial advisor is the same. A bad advisor could cause you to pay more in fees and taxes or even lose all of your money. Take the time to find advisors who can help you plan and achieveachieveachieve your financial goals in an efficient and effective way.

CHAPTER EIGHT

BEQUEATH A LEGACY

{ESTATE PLANNING}

How can someone leave a legacy? It means putting a stamp on the future and making a contribution to future generations. People want to leave a legacy because they want to feel that their life mattered.

Deciding what your legacy will be can help you withall ofall of all of the following:

You can start building your legacy once you know what you want it to be.

You can start by living the way you want to be remembered.

It will let you start doing the important things right away.

If you know what you want your legacy to be, you can use your time and other resources more wisely.

It will help you make good decisions in your daily life.

Figuring out what you want to be remembered for can give your life meaning and purpose.

It will give you the chance to let the legacy you're building shape how you act in the world every day.

You will live as if you are important.

Here are seven ways to figure out what kind of legacy you want to leave behind when you die.

What's your verse going to be?

The American movie Dead Poets Society takes place at a made-up elite conservative boarding school in Vermont in the year 1959. In the movie, Robin Williams plays John Keating, an English teacher who gets his students excited about writing poetry by teaching them about it.

In one scene, Keating has a conversation with his students about what life is all about. Keating says the following from the poem "Oh Me, Oh Life" by Walt Whitman:

"Oh, man! Of these questions that keep coming up, of the never-ending trains of the unfaithful, and of cities full of fools. What good is there in all this, me, life? Answer: "That you are here, which means that life and identity exist, that the powerful play goes on, and you can add a verse."

The poem says that life is like a play, and that everyone who has ever lived gets to write a verse. Then Keating asks the students, "What will your verse be?" " " Your legacy is the verse that you add to the play of life.

Think of yourself as a runner in a relay.

In a relay race, each member of a team runs while holding a baton in his or her hand. Each member of the team runs a part of the race, then passes the baton to the next runner. A relay race is one way to think about your life. President Barack Obama thinks of his life this way.

On May 25, 2010, Obama and German Chancellor Angela Merkel talked about democracy on May25th, 201025th, 2010 25th, 2010 in Berlin. Obama said the following about leaving a legacy:

"I saw myself as a runner on a relay team. I'd grab the baton and run my part of the race. Then I would pass the baton to the next person. person. person. Each generation tries to move forward, even though they know that what they do won't be perfect. But we hope that our part of the race went well and that the world is a little bit better because of it.

How's your part of the race going? Are you putting the baton forward? What are you doing to help the team move forward?

Imagine your 80th birthday.

Most of us have heard of the obituary exercise by Stephen Covey. Covey says that you should think about how you will die. Then, you should ask yourself questions like

Who would say something about you at your funeral?

What about you? Will? Will? Will they miss you?

What good things will they think of when they think of you?

What do they say about you?

Imagine your 80th birthday party instead of your funeral. It's a little morbid to think about your funeral, but it's a good way to do this

exercise. There is everyone you've had an effect on or influenced in some way. When they raise their glasses to toast you on your birthday, what would you like them to say about you birthday, what would you like them to say about you? You want your life to be about that.

What Do You Want Written on Your Gravestone?

Thomas Jefferson, the third president of the United States, told people what he wanted on his grave before he died. Jefferson wanted to have the following written on an obelisk:

This is where Thomas Jefferson was buried.

The man who wrote the Declaration of Independence

Of the Virginia Religious Freedom Statute

& the man who started the University of Virginia.

Most of us won't have tombstones nearly as impressive as Jefferson's. Still, an ordinary life lived well and with grace can make a big difference in other people's lives. What do you want to be written on your gravestone?

Questions to Ask Yourself About Leaving a Legacy

These 10 questions will help you figure out what you want to leave behind:

***What do you want to be known for in your life?**

*** How do you want your family and friends to remember you?**

***What will people outside of your family and close friends remember about you?**

***What kind of change do you want to make in your neighborhood?**

***How will your presence make the world a better place?**

*** How do you want to make a difference in your field?**

***How many people's lives will you have changed?**

***What lessons would you like to teach people who come after you?**

*** How do you want to be remembered?**

*** What can you do to help?**

20 Ways to Leave Something Behind

Use the following ideas as a starting point to come up with ways you can leave a mark:

1.

Learn more about your field.

2.

Leave something behind with your work.

3.

Publish a book.

4.

Leave money for your children and grandchildren that they can use to build their own financial futures.

5.

Give money to organizations that are important to you.

6.

Write down family recipes and the things you do as a family.

7.

The Act is a good example.

8.

Hand down a family treasure.

9.

Be a mentor.

10.

Volunteer

11.

Start a business or an organization that doesn't make money.

12.

Write your memoir. You can also record video messages for your loved ones, make a scrapbook for them, or make a website about your life.

13.

Give your old school a scholarship for future students.

14.

Write a legacy letter. Write down everything you'd want to say to your loved ones if you knew you didn't have long to live. Write about your life lessons, values, accomplishments, and hopes to

show who you really are. Think of it as a piece of your heart.

15.

Start a blog.

16.

Quilts, cedar hope chests, and wooden crafts are excellent items to pass down.Quilts, cedar hope chests, and wooden crafts are excellent items to pass down.Quilts, cedar hope chests, and wooden crafts are excellent items to pass down.

17.

Start a new program in your community, like a recycling program, a community garden, or a playground.

18.

Give people your skills and knowledge.

19.

Fix a mistake.

20.

Figure out what you're good at, improve your skills, and stay true to who you are.

Quotes about Leaving a Mark

Here are 10 quotes about leaving a legacy to give you more ideas:

"If you don't want to be forgotten after you die, do something worth writing about or write something worth reading," said Benjamin Franklin.

"To live forever is to do good things with your life and leave your mark," said Brandon Lee.

My grandfather said that when you die, you have to leave something behind. Something like a child, a book, a painting, a house, a wall, or a pair of shoes. Or a garden could be grown. Something you touched with your hand. Ray Bradbury, Fahrenheit 451,451,451,

"Our time is running out. One of our main goals in life should be to get ready for the day we die. What we leave behind is not just what we own, but also how well we lived. What plans should we make right now? " The most wasteful thing on earth, which can't be reused or recycled, is the time that God gives us each day." Bill Graham

Malloy smiled and said, "The little bit you and I might do to change the world wouldn't show up until a hundred years after we were gone. We'd never see it. But it would be there. James Jones, From Here to Eternity

WRITTEN AND DESIGNED BY

JOSE G KIM

www.ingramcontent.com/pod-product-compliance
Lightning Source LLC
LaVergne TN
LVHW050313160826
845677LV00014B/3371
9798849200200